Slip this card out
of this pocket page
for your
Snapshot Keepsake
Book instructions.

There's only one pretty child in the
world, and every mother has it.
—*Cheshire Proverb*

Designed and produced by Marquand Books, Inc.
Printed in Hong Kong

Endpaper photo courtesy of Utah State
Historical Society

Efforts have been made to find the copyright holders of
material used in this publication. We apologize for any
omissions or errors and will be pleased to include appropriate
acknowledgments in future editions.

ISBN 0-8118-0046-6

Distributed in Canada by Raincoast Books
112 East Third Avenue, Vancouver, B.C. V5T1C8

1 3 5 7 9 10 8 6 4 2

Chronicle Books
275 Fifth Street
San Francisco, CA 94103

My Baby

A Snapshot Keepsake Book

Michele Durkson Clise

CHRONICLE BOOKS

SAN FRANCISCO

**Every baby born into the world
is a finer one than the last.**
—Charles Dickens, 1839

Wee Babies

Babies short and babies tall,
Babies big and babies small,
Blue-eyed babies, babies fair,
Brown-eyed babies with lots of hair,
Babies so tiny they can't sit up,
Babies that drink from a silver cup,
Babies that coo and babies that creep,
Babies that only can eat and sleep,
Babies that laugh and babies that talk,
Babies quite big enough to walk,
Dimpled fingers and dimpled feet,
What in the world is half so sweet
As babies that jump, laugh, cry
 and crawl,
Eat, sleep, talk, walk, creep, coo
 and all,
Wee babies?

—Eugene Field (1850-1895)

A babe in a house is a
well-spring of pleasure.
—*M. F. Tupper, ca.1900*

Baby's Arrival

NAME

BIRTH DATE

TIME OF DAY

PLACE

WEIGHT

LENGTH

BABY'S FIRST DAYS

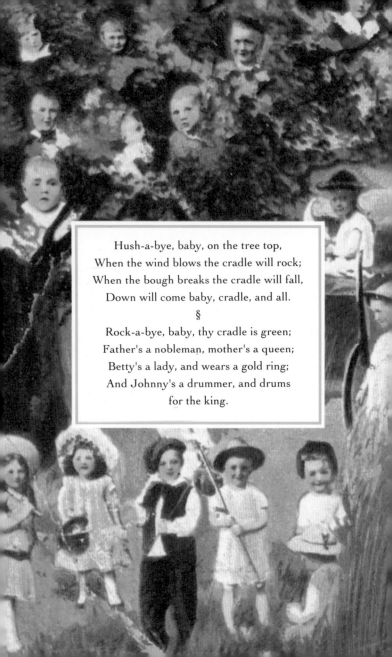

Hush-a-bye, baby, on the tree top,
When the wind blows the cradle will rock;
When the bough breaks the cradle will fall,
Down will come baby, cradle, and all.
§
Rock-a-bye, baby, thy cradle is green;
Father's a nobleman, mother's a queen;
Betty's a lady, and wears a gold ring;
And Johnny's a drummer, and drums
for the king.

Family Tree

MOTHER _____

FATHER _____

GRANDPARENTS _____

_____

SIBLINGS _____

OTHER RELATIVES _____

_____

_____

_____

_____

_____

_____

_____

Of all nature's gifts
to the human race,
what is sweeter to a man
than his children?
—*Cicero*

A B C D

E F G —

H I J K L

M N O P —

Q R S T U

and V

W X and Y

and Z

Firsts, Favorites & Feats

FIRST SMILE

_____

FIRST SOUNDS

_____

FIRST WORDS

_____

FIRST SIT-UP

_____

FIRST CRAWL

_____

FIRST SOLO STAND-UP

_____

FIRST STEP

_____

FIRST HAIRCUT

_____

FAVORITE TOYS

_____

_____

FAVORITE TUNE

_____

FAVORITE NURSERY RHYME

_____

AMAZING FEATS

_____

_____

Up in the air and over the wall,
Till I can see so wide,
Rivers and trees and cattle and all
Over the countryside—

Till I look down on the garden green;
Down on the roof so brown —
Up in the air I go flying again,
Up in the air and down!

—*Robert Louis Stevenson* (1850-1894)

A dash—and a splash—
A rinse—
and a rub—
You sailors! ahoy!
Don't rock the bath-tub!
You sailors! ahoy!
There—tip—goes the boat—
And the nursery floor
Is all afloat!

—*Anonymous, ca. 1900*

Baby's Friends

FIRST VISITORS

_____

_____

_____

FIRST PLAYMATES

_____

_____

_____

_____

_____

FIRST ANIMAL FRIENDS

_____

_____

_____

FAVORITE STUFFED ANIMALS

_____

_____

Pease porridge hot,
Pease porridge cold,
Pease porridge in the pot,
Nine days old.
Some like it hot,
Some like it cold,
Some like it in the pot,
Nine days old.

—*Nursery Rhyme*

Baby's Delights

Behold the child, by nature's kindly law,
Pleased with a rattle, tickled with a straw.

—Alexander Pope, 1732

FAVORITE NICKNAME

_____

FAVORITE BOOK

_____

_____

FAVORITE THING TO TAKE TO BED

_____

_____

FAVORITE GAMES

_____

_____

FAVORITE WORDS AND PHRASES

_____

_____

FUNNY THINGS THAT MAKE BABY SMILE

_____

_____

Said the child, "But I want one to play with—
oh I want a little yellow duck to take to bed with me."

—Jean Ingelow, ca. 1900

Happy those early days, when I
Shined in my angel-infancy.

—*Henry Vaughn, 1650*

Sweet babe, in thy face
Soft desires I can trace,
Secret joys and secret smiles,
Little pretty infant wiles.
—*William Blake (1757-1827)*

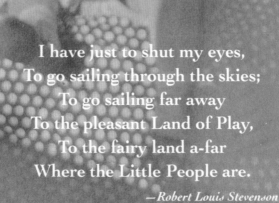

I have just to shut my eyes,
To go sailing through the skies;
To go sailing far away
To the pleasant Land of Play,
To the fairy land a-far
Where the Little People are.

—*Robert Louis Stevenson*

The Tyrant of the House

While baby sleeps
We cannot jump, or dance, or sing,
Play jolly games or do a thing
To make noise. The floor might creak
If we should walk! We scarcely speak
Or breathe while baby takes a nap,
Lest we should wake the little chap!
A strict watch Nursie always keeps
     While baby sleeps!

When baby wakes
But little gratitude he shows,
When other people want to doze!
At night, when folks have gone to bed,
He rouses them all up instead,
To wait on him. Ma lights the lamp.

And warms milk for the little scamp!
Pa walks him up and down the floor
Sometimes two hours and sometimes more!
And nurse comes running, in a stew,
To see what she for him can do!
And Will and Harry at the row
Call: "What's the matter with him now?"
And I'm waked up at all the clatter
To wonder what on earth's the matter!
Such uproar in the house he makes,
     When baby wakes!

So if asleep or if awake,
The house exists but for his sake,
And such a tiny fellow — he,
To be boss of this family!

                 —*Eva Lovett, ca. 1905*

To market, to market, to buy a plum bun,
Home again, home again, market is done.
—*Mother Goose*

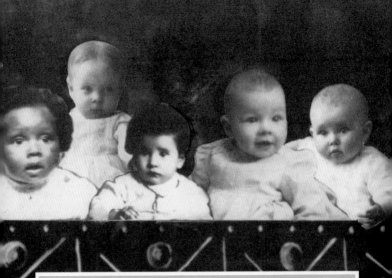

Baby's Trips & Travels

FIRST OUTINGS _____

_____

_____

FIRST SHORT TRIPS _____

_____

FIRST LONG TRIPS _____

_____

"Baby" around

Japanese	akambō
Czech	nemluvně
Finnish	lapsi
French	bébé
German	kleineskind
Italian	bambino

The World

Mandarin	yinghai
Norwegian	barn
Rumanian	copil
Russian	malyutka
Spanish	nene
Turkish	cocuk

Our Darling

Bounding like a football,
  Kicking at the door,
Falling from the table top —
  Sprawling on the floor.

Smashing cups and saucers,
  Splitting Dolly's head;
Putting little pussy cat
  Into baby's bed.

Building shops and houses,
  Spoiling father's hat,
Hiding mother's precious keys
  Underneath the mat.
Jumping on the fender,
  Poking at the fire,
Dancing on his little legs —
  Legs that never tire;
Making mother's heart leap
  Forty times a day —
Aping everything we do,
  Every word we say.

Shouting, laughing, tumbling,
  Roaring with a will;
Anywhere and everywhere,
  Never, never still;
Present — bringing sunshine;
  Absent — leaving night —
That's our precious darling,
  That's our heart's delight.

—Anonymous, ca. 1900

The Bee

What does the bee do?
Bring home honey.
And what does Father do?
Bring home money.
And what does Mother do?
Lay out the money.
And what does baby do?
Eat up the honey.

—*Christina Rossetti (1830-1894)*

Baby Food

FIRST SOLO DRINK FROM A BOTTLE
_____

FIRST SOLO DRINK FROM A CUP
_____

FIRST SOLO BITE FROM A SPOON
_____

_____

FAVORITE FOODS
_____

FAVORITE DRINKS
_____

FIRST SOLID FOODS
_____

_____

BABY'S FAVORITE FOOD GAMES
_____

_____

_____

_____

Pat-a-cake, pat-a-cake, baker's man!
So I will, master, as fast as I can:
Roll it, and prick it, and mark it with B,
And toss it in the oven for Baby and me.

While we were out the other day taking a stroll, I saw a nice little girl in short stockings. Her knees were all bare and they looked blue. I asked Mother about it and she said it was a FAD.

I don't know what she meant, but I am sure it is better for us to have on long stockings to keep our knees warm. I am glad Mother has not got a FAD; it must be a very bad thing to have.

Special Gifts for Baby

_____

_____

_____

_____

_____

_____

_____

_____

_____

_____

_____

_____

What use to me the gold and silver hoard?
What use to me the gems most rich and rare?
Brighter by far—
Ay! bright beyond compare—
The joys my children to my heart afford.

—*Yamagami no Okura (700-750)*

The Baby over the Way

The baby over the way, I know,
    Is a better baby than me;
For the baby over the way is all
    That a baby ought to be.

The baby over the way is neat,
    When I'm not fit to be seen;
His frock is smooth and his bib is sweet,
    And his ears are always clean.

He's wide awake when he's put to bed,
    But *he* never screams or cries;
He lies as still as a mouse, 'tis said,
    And closes his beautiful eyes.

He never wanted a comforter,
    Nor sips of tea from a spoon;
He never crumpled his pinafore,
    He never cried for the moon.

He's a dear little, sweet little angel bright,
    A love and a dove, they say;
But when I grow up, I am going to fight
    With the baby over the way!
        —*Fay Inchfawn, ca.1900*

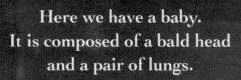

> Here we have a baby.
> It is composed of a bald head
> and a pair of lungs.
>
> —*Eugene Field, 1882*

As I look back on those distant days and nights I am sorry that I was so fretty, yet I really think that I made no more fuss than father did when he had a toothache. He said some wicked words that I hadn't learned yet. I relieved my feelings in the only way I could—by crying. I am sure that we babies deserve to be treated with great patience. We hold it in just as long as we can. It is no fun to cut teeth.

Baby Grumbles

DATES OF FIRST TEETH

VACCINATIONS AND INOCULATIONS

BIGGEST COMPLAINTS

MAJOR PUBLIC TANTRUMS

HABITS I LIKE BUT GROWN-UPS DON'T

If all the world were apple-pie,
And all the sea were ink,
And all the trees were bread and cheese,
What should we have for drink?
—*Mother Goose*

Don't set your wit against a child.
—Jonathan Swift, 1738

Advice to Baby's Sitter

_____

_____

_____

In Case of an Emergency

_____

_____

_____